There's a Babirusa in My Bathtub!

Fact and Fancy About Curious Creatures

By Maxine Rose Schur • Illustrated by Michael S. Maydak

Dawn Publications

S0-AZR-093

DEDICATIONS

For Sebastian, my grandson and my very favorite little boy. — MRS
To Wolf and Teal, may you explore the uniqueness of the world. — MSM

Acknowledgment: Thanks to Carol L. Malnor who generously gave her advice and assistance in the development of the activities for teachers and parents. — MRS

Copyright © 2009 Maxine Rose Schur

A Sharing Nature With Children Book

All rights reserved. No part of this book may be reproduced or transmitted to any form or by any means, electronic or mechanical, including photocopying, recording, or by any information and retrieval system, without written permission from the publisher.

Library of Congress Cataloging-in-Publication Data
Schur, Maxine.
  There's a babirusa in my bathtub! : fact and fancy about curious creatures / by Maxine Schur ; Illustrated by Michael S. Maydak. -- 1st ed.
    p. cm.
  "Witty poems about remarkable but little-known creatures are accompanied by illustrations and narrative descriptions of the animals. Activities designed to assist reading teachers are also included" - Provided by the publisher.
  ISBN 978-1-58469-117-4 (hardback) -- ISBN 978-1-58469-118-1 (pbk.) 1. Animals--Miscellanea--Juvenile literature. 2. Babirusa--Juvenile literature. I. Maydak, Michael S., ill. II. Title.
  QL49.S2737 2009
  590--dc22
                        2008038514

Printed in China
10 9 8 7 6 5 4 3 2 1
First Edition

Design and computer production by Patty Arnold, Menagerie Design and Publishing
The font Sketch Rockwell was designed by Lukas Bischoff www.artill.de

Dawn Publications
12402 Bitney Springs Road
Nevada City, CA 95959
530-274-7775
nature@dawnpub.com

You've
heard of cats and you've
heard of bats
And giraffes and zebras, of course.
You've heard of
birds and know so
many words
For creatures
like the elephant,
fox and horse.

But outside a zoo,
what would you do
With an animal you didn't
know?
Do you think you'd be
frightened?
Or want to be enlightened?
If so... turn these pages and go!

Babirusa

(bab-uh- ROO-suh)

There's a babirusa in my bathtub.
I sure wish he'd get out.
I'd fight with him about it
But he's got tusks on his snout.

There's a babirusa in my bathtub
And I wish he'd go away,
But he looks so very fearful
I'm much too scared to say
"GO AWAY!"

He's splashing all the water
And making a big mess.
Yet when he asks me if I like it
I answer "YES! YES! YES!"

The babirusa would never leave your bathtub because it loves water. It especially loves to swim long distances. In its great hunt for food, a babirusa will swim from one island to another!

People in Indonesia call the babirusa a pig-deer because it has legs like a deer and a face like a pig. And what a face! The babirusa has the strangest tusks. The top pair grows upward and curves backwards, sometimes piercing the skin of its face. The lower pair sticks out between the lips and also curves upwards. These four big tusks make the babirusa look more dangerous than it really is.

Babirusas live in groups of about eight. A group of babirusas is called a "troop." In the heat of the day, a troop spends its time wallowing in cool mud. At night the male babirusas use their unusual tusks to dig up the ground. When they uncover a root or a nut, they give out a happy groan. The males give the female babirusas and their babies the first chance to eat whatever is found.

Fabulous Fact

To prove who is strongest, male babirusas stand on their hind legs and box each other.

Civet

(SIV-it)

Tangling with a tangalung?
Mangling!

Wrangling with a delandung?
Jangling!

Brawling with a binturong?
Wrong!

Scrapping with sulawezi?
Crazy!

Advice:

DON'T PLAY WRANGLED,
   TANGLED GAMES
WITH CATS WHO HAVE
   NEW-FANGLED NAMES

The tangalung, delandung, binturong and sulawezi are all names for different civets that live in the jungles of Africa and Asia. And that's not all. There's also the linsang, musang, falouka, fossa and others! There are many kinds of civets but not every one has a tongue-twisting name. The civet in the illustration, for example, is simply called the "banded palm" civet. Civets are often called "cats" but they are not really cats. Look closely and you see a civet has a weasel-like face and raccoon tail.

Civits are best known for their smell. This animal has a gland that makes a smelly liquid called musk. When the civet sprays its territory with musk, other civets stay away. For more than a hundred years, the musk did not keep people away. It was the musk itself that people wanted! Why? When musk is added to perfume, it makes the perfume smell nice longer. Today people make artificial musk and it works just as well. That's good news for the lovely tangalung, delandung, binturong, and sulawezi, not to mention the linsang, musang, falouka, fossa, and other tongue-twisting civets.

Fabulous Fact

The musang is a civet that loves to drink the sap from the palm tree. The sap has a lot of alcohol in it. People make the sap into a drink called "toddy." Sometimes musangs will drink so much sap that they get drunk and fall out of trees. That's why they're nicknamed "toddy cats."

Colugo

(kuh-LOO-go)

Colugo clings to tree trunks tight
Until the dark advance of night,
When shaping himself like a kite
Colugo launches into flight.

With spread-cloak skin in a single
    bound
He glides above the jungle ground.
From tree to tree and all around
He soars without the slightest sound.

But with the light of a brand new day,
Just like putting a toy away,
Colugo folds up small and gray,
For on a tree trunk he must stay.

Silent, still, out of sight
Until the dark advance of night.

This cat-size animal lives in the rainforests of Southeast Asia. During the day, the colugo sleeps clinging to a tree trunk. You might think it looks very boring—like a burst balloon.

But wait.

At night the colugo spreads its skin wide and takes off! It sails from tree to tree, searching for fruit, flowers and leaves. It does not fly like a bat or a bird. It sails on waves of air, like a hang glider. And like a hang glider, the colugo steers through the air with just slight movements of its body.

The colugo is at home in the rainforest but only in the trees. If a colugo is put on the ground, it can barely move, for it is unable to walk.

The colugo's teeth are unique. Each tooth is shaped like a comb. The colugo uses its teeth to comb its fur and to dig sweet sap out of tree trunks. Everything about the colugo is unusual, including the noise it makes—like a duck quacking!

Fabulous Fact

Often, colugos share a tree that's particularly good for launching their flight. They line up for take-off like airplanes on a runway.

Dingo

(DING-goh)

Never play a game of bingo
With the sly Australian dingo.
It's not that he's so fond of cheating
But rather that he's fond of eating.

His teeth are sharp as blades of
    steel—
A fact to know and not to feel.
He doesn't care a bit for fair play.
Should he lose, then I daresay
You might think you are the winner
When, in fact, you are the dinner.

No, never play a game of bingo
With the sly Australian dingo.
But if you choose it ...

Lose it.

The dingo may look like a dog, but don't pet it! The dingo is fearless and will attack animals much larger than itself. And yes, it is fond of eating—especially sheep. The dingo is native to Australia where the sheep farmers view the dingo as a terrible threat. No wonder; a pack of eight dingoes can kill more than 200 sheep in one night. To protect their flocks, the sheep farmers built the longest fence in the world to keep this wild dog out. The fence is 3,500 miles long!

Though the dingo looks like a dog, it is very different. A dingo cannot move its ears or wag its tail. Instead of barking, the dingo lets out an eerie howl. However, if raised from birth with dogs, it will imitate a dog's bark.

Fabulous Fact

A mother dingo feeds her pups by vomiting her latest meal into their mouths. Seconds, anyone?

Hagfish

(HAG-fish)

When a flirty hagfish
Feels like a dirty ragfish,
She ties herself into a bow
And squeezes clean from head to roe.
This crazy bath appeals to eels
Who brag about how nice it feels.
Recently some children tried it.
Though these children have denied it.

You, yourself might want to try.
You might like it or . . .
You might knot.

Though the hagfish is not really an eel, it is also called the slime eel, the blind eel and even the snot eel. It has no fins, no scales, and no jaws. It has eyes that cannot see, and only a tiny mouth surrounded by long whiskers. The hagfish lurks at the bottom of the ocean, buried up to its snout.

To move through the mud, the hagfish's body makes slime. The slime is called mucus and it's a little like the stuff that comes out of your nose when you have a cold. The hagfish makes a lot of it. How much? A hagfish can turn a large bucket of water into slime in just minutes! The slime is useful. When a hagfish is caught, the slime allows it to slip away. When the hagfish is hungry, the slime chokes all the fish around, making them easy to catch. But often the slime becomes too much even for the hagfish itself. The slime gets up its nostril (it has just one), making it sneeze. When the hagfish gets too slimy, it ties itself into a knot which travels down its body, squeezing out the slime.

The hagfish has a strange tongue for it's completely lined with teeth! In just one hour, a hagfish can eat more than its own weight of dead fish it finds on the ocean floor.

Fabulous Fact

Though a hagfish can eat an enormous amount of food, it can also eat very little, even nothing. A hagfish can go up to seven months without eating anything!

Jerboa

(jur-BO-ah)

When all the animals were in the ark
The good Lord said to Noah,
"You've got the dog; you've got the frog,
But where is that little jerboa?

"You've got the horse and the cow,
   of course
And snakes from python to boa.
I see a goose, and a duck on the loose
But where is that little jerboa?

"You've got the rat and sly old cat
And you've got that big bird, the moa.
There's enough in your ark for a
   zoological park
But where is that little jerboa?"

Noah searched every inch of his ark
And all the animals helped Noah.
They looked in the boxes and then
Near the foxes, they found that little
   jerboa.

And the Lord said: "Noah, Now, you
   can goah."

The jerboa is so tiny you have to look hard to find it. Once you find it, you have to look quickly. The jerboa can jump faster than you can run. Some jerboas, no bigger than your fist, can jump 12 feet in one flying leap. Using its tufted tail for steering, the jerboa can even change course mid-flight! This Olympic skill helps the jerboa dodge danger instantly. It also helps when it hunts for insects at night.

The jerboa lives in the deserts of North Africa and Central Asia. Like many rodents, it lives on seeds, grasses and insects. During the hot day, it stays in its underground hole which it plugs up with earth to keep in the moisture. Here, the jerboa sleeps standing up and rolled forward into a ball. It gets pretty cramped like this, so when it wakes up the first thing the jerboa does is leave the hole, stretch, and roll around in the sand. Ahhhhh.

Fabulous Fact

The jerboa has thick hair on the pads of its feet that absorb the shock of landing after its gigantic jumps.

Kinkajou

(KING-kuh-joo)

A kinkajou doesn't think of you
As she goes about her day.
You needn't exist
For you're not even missed,
Her mind is so far away.

It might just appall you
That she doesn't call you
Let alone send you
Hugs or money.

But you won't take it so hard
That you don't get a card
When you learn that her mind
Is on
Honey.

The kinkajou is often called a "honey bear." It is not a bear but it does have strong claws, round ears and thick fur, and like a bear, it loves honey. Sometimes the honey drips all over its face and fur. The kinkajou always looks like it is having fun! It lives in the tree tops of the rainforests of Central America and jumps noisily from tree to tree. It also sucks nectar out of flowers and feasts on bugs, mice and birds.

The kinkajou hunts at night, and has excellent vision. If a light shines onto its gigantic eyes, they will seem to glow and can be seen from very far away. During the day, the kinkajou sleeps inside a hollow tree. Male kinkajous like to hang from their long tails upside down and playfully box one another in the head.

Kinkajous have a nature just as sweet as the honey they eat. Although they are messy eaters, they make very nice pets!

Fabulous Fact

The kinkajou makes a variety of noises. It can chirp and whistle like a bird, yelp like a dog, huff, shriek and even whisper.

Loris

(LAW-ris)

There's a loris in our chorus
Who's truly roly-poly,
And that loris in our chorus
Is singing much too slowly.

We've begged him to sing quicker,
To liven up his pace,
But all he does is bicker,
Saying, "Singing's not a race."

There's a loris in our chorus
Who is really fat and furry.
And that loris in our chorus
Is impossible to hurry!

This animal really sings, and it does everything slowly. In fact the full name for some species of loris is "slow loris." Native to the jungles of Southeast Asia, the loris likes to sing to other lorises in a high-pitched voice. But if startled, the loris will open its mouth wide and let out a scary, buzzing sound.

It moves hand over hand slowly through the tops of the trees—so slowly that the leaves do not even move as it passes by.

During the day, the loris tucks its head and arms between its legs and sleeps holding on to a branch with a powerful grip. It looks like a big ball of fur. At night the loris hunts insects, lizards and bird eggs. When the loris is thirsty, it simply touches a wet leaf then sucks the water from its fingers. Easy.

Fabulous Fact

The loris is named for its funny face. The word "loris" comes from the Dutch word for clown.

Manatee

(MAN-uh-tee)

Should you spot a manatee
Don't think you've lost your sanity.
The odds of seeing one are rare,
But if you do, it's really there.
The manatee is just as real
As a turtle, fish, or seal.
So move in for a closer look
Or learn about it from a book.
Then should you spot the sleek
   dugong
You know you will not get it wrong,
And mistake a manatee for his
   cousin.
Yes, even if you spot a dozen
You'll know the fact that never fails:

ONLY MANATEES HAVE SPOON-
SHAPED TAILS.

Manatees and dugongs are large marine mammals. They are more related to elephants than to whales or dolphins. They are as big as cows. Like cows, they travel in herds, produce milk and graze on grass—sea grass that grows underwater. The manatee swims along the coast of Florida, South America and Africa. It is gentle and likes to play. It's fun to watch a manatee body surf and do barrel rolls!

The dugong is a close relative of the manatee, living in the coastal waters of Australia.

Can you tell them apart? Of course you can! The manatee has a rounded tail like a beaver's. The dugong's tail is split like a whale's or like the mermaid's. In fact, because dugongs are sleek and graceful, some early sailors thought dugongs were mermaids.

Manatees and dugongs belong to the species, *sirenia*. Because they are mammals, they need to come up often for air, but when they are excited, they dive deep and let out a loud whistle! And this is how we got the word "siren."

Fabulous Fact

Manatees like to play "follow the leader." They sometimes move in a single file and coordinate their movements such as breathing, diving and changing direction like synchronized swimmers!

Matamata

(MA-ta-MA-ta)

Matamata waiting all alone,
Looking like a leafy stone.
Along comes a fish and bites his back
Thinking leaves are a tasty snack.

ATTACK!
THE SNACK BITES BACK!

That hapless fish is swallowed quick!
And this was matamata's trick:
Making that hungry, hasty fish
Think matamata was the tasty dish.

The matamata is a very tricky turtle. Its shell is made up of many skin flaps shaped like leaves and covered with algae. These flaps sway and drift with the water currents. The matamata looks as if it is a plant of green leaves. In South America, at the bottom of the Amazon River, the matamata sits without moving until a fish comes along and tries to nibble on a leaf. With lightening speed, the matamata stretches its long neck and swallows the fish whole.

Matamata has other ways of catching fish. This turtle walks along the river, herding fish as it goes! The matamata corners them against a rock then sucks them up with its big mouth— as swiftly as a vacuum cleaner.

Unlike other turtles, matamatas never bask in the sun and they are poor swimmers. Their breathing is different too. They breathe by extending their neck so that their long snout sticks up above the water. This makes them look as if they are snorkeling!

Fabulous Fact

The matamata has frills on its neck. The frills detect even slight movements of water. In this way the frills let the matamata know there's a fish nearby so it can get ready to attack.

Okapi

(oh-KAH-pee)

Authentic
Beautiful
Curious
Different
Extraordinary
First
Genuine
Handsome
Individual
Jungle-dwelling
Kind
Lone
Magnificent
Novel
Original
Particular

Quirky
Rare
Special
Terrific
Unique
Vital
Weird
Xceptional
Yellow-eared
Zebra-striped

Okapi
No Copy.

The okapi is really one of a kind. What other animal do you know that has purplish fur, a striped behind, and a tongue that is long enough to clean its ears? The okapi is related to the giraffe. It looks like a cross between a zebra and a horse. It is not as tall as a giraffe: it stands about as high as a pony.

The okapi lives in only one place in the world: in the dark and damp Ituri rainforest, located in the Democratic Republic of the Congo. It eats the lower leaves of the trees.

The okapi is a shy, gentle animal. It moves about alone, silently blending into the deep shadows of the forest. In this quiet, secretive way, it keeps out of sight of leopards. The okapi has survived for centuries because it is so hard to see. The colors of the okapi are the same colors and patterns of the dark forest in which it lives. You could be standing very close to an okapi and not even see it!

The okapi was discovered in 1901. It was the last mammal to be discovered by scientists in the 20th century. In the thick forest, the okapi is so well hidden that we hardly know more about it today than we did one hundred years ago. Wouldn't you like to know more?

Fabulous Fact

If a giraffe invited all its relatives to its birthday party, the okapi would be the only guest.

Tamandua

(ta-MAN-dyo-uh)

I've got ants on my fingers,
Got termites on my tongue,
But I've never been bit,
I've never been stung!

Why don't you come and try it?
Lots of crawlies for your lunch.
It's a really tasty diet,
Eating bugs by the bunch!

And… then… you'll sing…

I've got ants on my fingers,
Got termites on my tongue,
But I've never been bit,
I've never been stung!

Why don't you come and try it?
Lots of crawlies for your lunch.
It's a really tasty diet,
Eating bugs by the bunch!

How would you like to be called "stinker of the forest"? No? Well, that's the name that the local people in the Amazon rainforest give to the tamandua. When a tamandua feels threatened by another animal, its glands produce a nasty smell. It's a smell that would make you run and leave it alone.

The tamandua is a type of anteater that lives in Central and South America. Its nose is long and so is its powerful tail by which it hangs from a tree branch. But its mouth is as tiny as the eraser on your pencil! The tamandua doesn't need a big mouth because what it eats is very small: termites, grubs, bees, and ants.

The saliva in the tamandua's mouth is super-sticky. The tamandua can drop its very long tongue 16 inches down a termite hole and reel it up with hundreds of termites stuck to it. Tamanduas lick their paws to make them sticky so they can easily pick up ants and just lick them off their fingers. Yum.

Fabulous Fact

Tamanduas never destroy a whole ant or termite nest. They eat only a portion of the colony, then move on to the next one. By preserving the colonies, they ensure their future food.

Tasmanian Devil

(taz-MEY-nee-un)

Those folks who named me "Devil"
Did not use their brains!
I'm really not as devilish
As everybody claims.
This bad name
Appalls me!
It absolutely galls me!

MAKES ME WANT TO BITE YOU!
FEROCIOUSLY FIGHT YOU!
TO MUNCH AND CRUNCH!
AND EAT YOU UP FOR LUNCH!

So I'm sure you won't mind
Since I'm really so kind,
Renaming me,
and claiming me
TASMANIAN ANGEL.

Have you seen Taz, the Tasmanian Devil in a Bugs Bunny cartoon? If so, you haven't seen the Tasmanian Devil at all! The real Tasmanian Devil looks nothing like the cartoon character. It looks like a cross between a dog and a cat. It also looks scarier because it is scarier. This animal is only the size of a small dog but is as fierce as a tiger.

The Tasmanian Devil lives on the Australian island of Tasmania. With its huge, powerful jaws it will eat anything. It devours both live and dead animals of any kind, eating all bones, fur and feathers. A Tasmanian Devil will even eat another Tasmanian Devil!

The Devil's black fur is a great camouflage when it hunts for food at night. When threatened, it gives off a really bad smell and becomes vicious. To top it off, the animal opens its enormous mouth and sends out a terrifying sound. It starts like a loud whistle and ends in a spine-chilling screech and... what? You're going back to the cartoon?

Fabulous Fact

The Tasmanian Devil prefers to eat already dead animals. Because it eats the entire animal, the Devil helps to prevent the spread of disease.

Wait—There's more!

You've met strange animals from cover to cover.

Now, how many more can you discover?

Here is a nice alphabetical list

Of other rare animals not to be missed!

Aye Aye	Numbat
Bilby	Oryx
Capybara	Pichiciago
Duiker	Quagga
Eland	Ratel
Falanaka	Saiga
Guanaco	Tamarin
Hyrax	Unau
Indri	Vicuna
Javelina	Wombat
Kowari	Xenopus
Langur	Yapok
Muntjac	Zoril

There are many more little-known animals. In fact, new ones are being discovered all the time. Scientists estimate that many thousands of species have yet to be identified—especially ones living in the oceans. Pick an animal, find out about it, and tell your friends about it.

Hidden Pictures— Accept the Challenge!

There's a picture hidden in every main illustration—actually, very well hidden! Can you find it? The picture refers to something mentioned in the poem or in the text.

Babirusa:	Boxing glove
Civet:	Scrabble pieces spelling out BINTURONG
Colugo:	Airplane on a runway
Dingo:	Dog bowl with the name Dingo on it
Hagfish:	Boy Scout merit badge for knots
Jerboa:	Olympic medal for the high jump
Kinkajou:	Honey pot
Loris:	Clown face
Manatee:	Mermaid
Matamata:	Neon sign that says "Fast Food"
Okapi:	Birthday party hat
Tamandua:	Pencil
Tasmanian Devil:	Whistle

What's In a Name?

Using the Okapi poem as a model, pick a name of any animal and write its attributes using the letters that make up that animal's name. For example: Jerboa

Jumping
Energetic
Rolling
Bouncy
Olympic skill
African

Ghostwriters

(A comprehension activity)

Choose an animal and then write a postcard that that animal might send to your class. Even better, use a 3x5 card to create a real postcard with a photo or drawing on one side and writing on the other—combining writing and art, just as this book does. Here are some ideas:

What would the animal say it was doing?

What would make a good day for the animal?

A bad day?

What would the animal's return address be?

How would the animal describe the food where it lives?

The scenery?

The other animals?

The sounds it hears?

Rhyme Twins

(A fluency, phonics and phonemic awareness activity)

Pick a poem and read it aloud until you can easily pronounce all of the words. Then read it to a partner. Have your partner listen for "rhyme twins"—two (or more) words that rhyme with each other. Then write them down. It's especially fun when words can be spelled very differently yet still rhyme, such as "tongue" and "stung." Examples can be found throughout the book. Then create a simple two-line poem about a different animal, especially an animal that lives near where you live, using the same rhyming words.

Sounds Like

(A phonics activity)

Suggestion for teachers: write the names of the animals on the board. As you read aloud each name, point out phonics patterns, such as the two different ways the letter "c" is pronounced in coqui and civet, and the two ways the letter "a" is pronounced in matamata and okapi. Then have children take turns reading the animal names to a partner.

Dingoes and Dogs

(A comprehension and graphic organizing activity)

Suggestion for teachers: have readers form pairs. Assign two animals to each pair, choosing one animal from the book plus one locally familiar animal. Ask partners to make a list of how their animals are the same and how they are different. Have them use their lists to create a Venn diagram, which can be posted on a bulletin board.

Fact or Fancy?

(A comprehension and graphic organizing activity)

Suggestion for teachers: on a chalkboard or a piece of paper make a table with two columns, one titled "fact" (or "real") and one titled "fancy" (or "make believe," or "fiction"). Ask the children to identify which things about an animal are real and which things are fancy, and list in the appropriate column. What clues in the book help them tell the difference? This is especially good as a small-group activity in which each group gets an animal. Each group can conclude by sharing their most "unusual fact" and most "outrageous fancy" with the whole class.

Word Wall

(A vocabulary and comprehension activity)

Suggestion for teachers: create a Word Wall by posting the names of all the curious creatures on a wall or bulletin board. Underneath each name, post a 3x5 card for each new vocabulary word found in the poem or passage. Have the vocabulary word written on the front of the card and the definition written on the back. Ask children to read about an animal and use the context to write down a possible definition for each new vocabulary word. When finished, have them look at the back of the card to read the correct definition. Then have them read the poem and passage again.

MAXINE ROSE SCHUR is an award-winning travel essayist and the author of several critically-acclaimed books for children, including historical novels, biography and picture books. Maxine lives in the San Francisco Bay Area. To learn more about her books, writing classes and speaking engagements, go to www.maxineroseschur.com.

Photo by David Sanger

MICHAEL S. MAYDAK is a professional artist who is passionate about nature—especially the riparian environments that he loves so much as a fly fisherman. Mike is an art graduate of San Jose University and has been a professional artist since 1976, with his studio at his home in Cool, California. This is the sixth book he has illustrated for Dawn Publications.

A FEW OTHER BOOKS FROM DAWN PUBLICATIONS

Eliza and the Dragonfly by Susie Rinehart, illustrated by Anisa Claire Hovemann, is a charming story revolving around the beauty and wonder of the hidden world that can be found in a local pond.

The Web at Dragonfly Pond by Brian "Fox" Ellis, illustrated by Michael S. Maydak—a real-life story of fishing with father that reveals how nature's food chain is connected.

If You Give a T-Rex a Bone by Tim Myers, illustrated by Anisa Claire Hovemann. So you'd like to go back in time and see a T-Rex? That would be very cool. Along the way you're bound to encounter many other wild and amazing creatures from the past.

Earth's Heroes: Champions of the Wilderness by Bruce and Carol Malnor, illustrated by Anisa Claire Hovemann, features the youth, careers and lasting contributions of some of the world's greatest naturalists and environmentalists. This volume, the first in a series of three, includes eight people, from historic greats John Muir and Aldo Leopold, to such current luminaries as David Suzuki and Wangari Maathai.

How We Know What We Know About Our Changing Climate by Lynne Cherry and Gary Braasch is the award-winning book that with great clarity presents the science behind the headlines—evidence from flowers, butterflies, birds, frogs, trees and much more. The overall tone is urgent without being shrill, hopeful without being complacent.

The Universe series by Jennifer Morgan, illustrated by Dana Lynne Andersen, presents the amazing story of the Universe—science in an exceedingly understandable and lively package, narrated by . . . the Universe itself.

Born With a Bang: The Universe Tells Our Cosmic Story
From Lava to Life: The Universe Tells Our Earth Story
Mammals Who Morph: The Universe Tells Our Evolution Story

Dawn Publications is dedicated to inspiring in children a deeper understanding and appreciation for all life on Earth. To view our titles or to order, please visit us at www.dawnpub.com, or call 800-545-7475.